✳ Smithsonian

GIANT SQUID

SEARCHING FOR A SEA MONSTER

by Mary M. Cerullo with Clyde F. E. Roper

CAPSTONE PRESS
a capstone imprint

Capstone Press
1710 Roe Crest Drive
North Mankato, Minnesota 56003
www.capstonepub.com

 Books published by Capstone Press are manufactured with paper
containing at least 10 percent post-consumer waste.

The name of the Smithsonian Institution and the sunburst logo are registered trademarks of the
Smithsonian Institution. For more information, please visit www.si.edu.

Library of Congress Cataloging-in-Publication Data
Cerullo, Mary M.
 Giant squid : searching for a sea monster / by Mary M. Cerullo with Clyde F.E. Roper.
   p. cm. — (Smithsonian)
 Includes bibliographical references and index.
 Summary: "Describes the science of the giant squid and the challenges in finding and
learning about this cephalopod"—Provided by publisher.
 ISBN 978-1-4296-7541-3 (library binding)
 ISBN 978-1-4296-8023-3 (paperback)
 1. Giant squids—Juvenile literature. I. Roper, Clyde F. E., 1937– II. Title. III. Series.
 QL430.3.A73C47 2012
 594'.58—dc23

                                        2011029181

Editorial Credits: Kristen Mohn, editor; Sarah Bennett, designer; Deirdre Barton, media researcher;
Laura Manthe, production specialist

Our very special thanks to Michael Vecchione at the National Museum of Natural History for his curatorial
review. Capstone would also like to thank Ellen Nanney and Kealy Wilson at the Smithsonian Institution's
Office of Product Development and Licensing for their help in the creation of this book.

Smithsonian Enterprises: Carol LeBlanc, Vice President; Brigid Ferraro, Director of Licensing

Photo Credits: Cathy and Bob Cranston/Bob Cranston, 29 (Clyde) • Clyde F.E. Roper, PhD, or Ingrid
Roper, front cover, bc cover, 9 (shark skin)/Washington Post, 11 (girl), 12 (Clyde), 15 (whale), 18, 19, 22,
23 (Clyde), 24, 30 (ship), 31 (crittercam), 33, 34 (AUV, art), 36, 37 (Deep Rover), 48 (Clyde) • Corbis/
Stefano Bianchetti, 6 • Getty Images/Hulton Archive, 4/DEA Picture Library, 6–7/Dorling Kindersley, 8–9,
35 (art)/Jeff Rotman, 35 (fishermen) • Dr. James Mead/Smithsonian Institution, 7 (ambergris) • Mary Evans
Picture Library, 11 (art) • Mary M. Cerullo, 48 (Mary) • National Geographic Stock/Greg Marshall, 30–31
(penguin) • National Museum of Natural History/Smithsonian Institution, 13 (diagram)/Dr. Richard Young/
University of Honolulu/Smithsonian Institution, 23 (statoliths)/John Steiner/Smithsonian Institution, 44 •
Courtesy of the Peabody Museum of Natural History, 10 • Peter Milholland, 12 (snail) • Photo Researchers,
Inc/Science Photo Library/Richard Ellis, 1, 2–3/Sinclair Stammers, 9 (beak) • Sea Pics/Masa Ushioda, 14,
15 (octopus)/Jez Tryner, 15 (cuttlefish)/Richard Dirscherl, 15 (squid)/John C. Lewis, 20 (calamari)/David
B. Fleetham, 20 (oval)/David Wrobe, 20 (glass)/Eric Cheng, 21/Peter Parks, 25/Ethan Daniels, 26/Franco
Banfi, 27, 28–29/Mark Conlin, 29 (beak), 35 (coral)/Kat Bolstad, 30 (scientist)/James D. Watt, 32/Richard
Ellis, 37 (art)/Andrew J. Martinez, 38 • Tsunemi Kubodera/Japan's National Science Museum 39 (diagram),
40, 41, 42, 43 • Shutterstock, 5, 7 (bird), 9 (sketch), 13 (nudibranch), 16, 17, 18–19 (background), 22
(background), 24–25 (art), 30–31 (background), 33 (art), 34 (plate), 39 (map), 45, 47

*Note about websites: At the time of printing, all websites in this book were
correct and suitable for our readers.*

Printed in the United States of America in North Mankato, Minnesota.
102011   006405CGS12

Dedications

To Cindy Hibbert, Jill McMahon, and Tina Armstrong,
for friendships that endure—M.C.

To Ingrid, who has supported my work throughout my
entire career, as a partner on many expeditions, and as
editor and technical adviser in my writing and teaching.
For all of this assistance I am eternally grateful.—C.F.E.R.

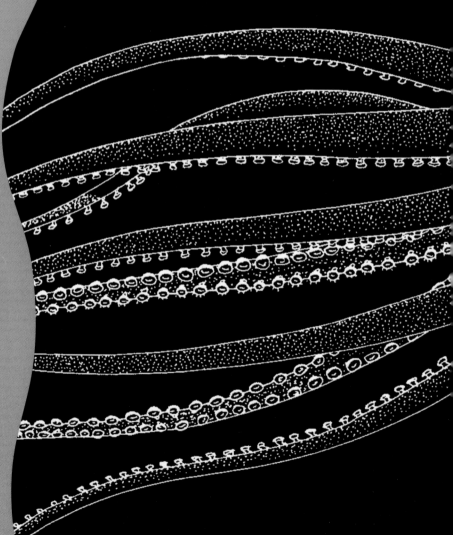

Contents

4

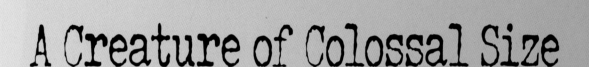

A Creature of Colossal Size

Without warning, a gigantic, twisting tentacle bursts out of a dark sea. As flexible as a human hand, it snatches a sailor from the deck of his ship. A single scream pierces the night. The sailor and the creature are gone.

When the seas were still largely uncharted, sailors and fishermen told stories like this about a mythic monster of the deep. Norwegian sailors described a spiderlike creature as big as an island. Its long arms could wrap around the masts of a ship and drag it to the bottom of the ocean. Or the monster could create a gigantic whirlpool as it dove back into the depths, pulling the ship down with it.

Sailors and storytellers called the creature the *kraken*. Drawings of this mysterious beast bore a strong resemblance to what we now know as the giant squid.

In 1874 a newspaper account of an actual encounter between a ship's crew and a giant sea creature inspired the French author Jules Verne to revise a book he was writing. As the paper reported, a sea captain claimed that he had ordered his crew to fire on a many-armed sea monster, which he believed was trying to climb aboard his ship. Riddled with rifle bullets and weighed down by cannonballs, the beast finally sank beneath the waves.

Verne put this tale to work in his fiction. An attack on Captain Nemo and the crew of the *Nautilus* by a "squid of colossal size" became the most famous scene in Verne's book *Twenty Thousand Leagues Under the Sea.*

5

Early Clues

Eventually these bizarre creatures—or at least evidence of them—began to show up in more than just seafarers' tales. In the 1700s and 1800s, many captains of whaling ships were amateur naturalists—people who study nature. They recorded what they observed in their ships' logs. Some of these captains hunted sperm whales, the largest toothed whales that ever lived. When they hauled their catch on board, they often noticed strange circular scars on the whale's head and jaws. These scars suggested a fierce wrestling match with some enormous beast. But what creature could take on a 70-ton whale?

In 1861 a French warship encountered a "sea monster." The sailors harpooned it several times but only succeeded in hauling up the back end of the beast. However, that was enough to identify their prize as a giant squid.

Inside the stomachs of the whales was another mystery: waxy balls of a smelly substance called ambergris. These oily lumps are made by the digestive juices of whales. Ambergris coats any hard object a whale swallows that could irritate its stomach. In the center of the lumps, sailors found what looked like large birds' beaks.

beaks

mm 50 55 60 65 70 75 80 85 90 95 100

Fresh ambergris from a whale's stomach stinks, but over time it mellows into an attractive fragrance used in expensive perfumes.

Did sperm whales eat birds?

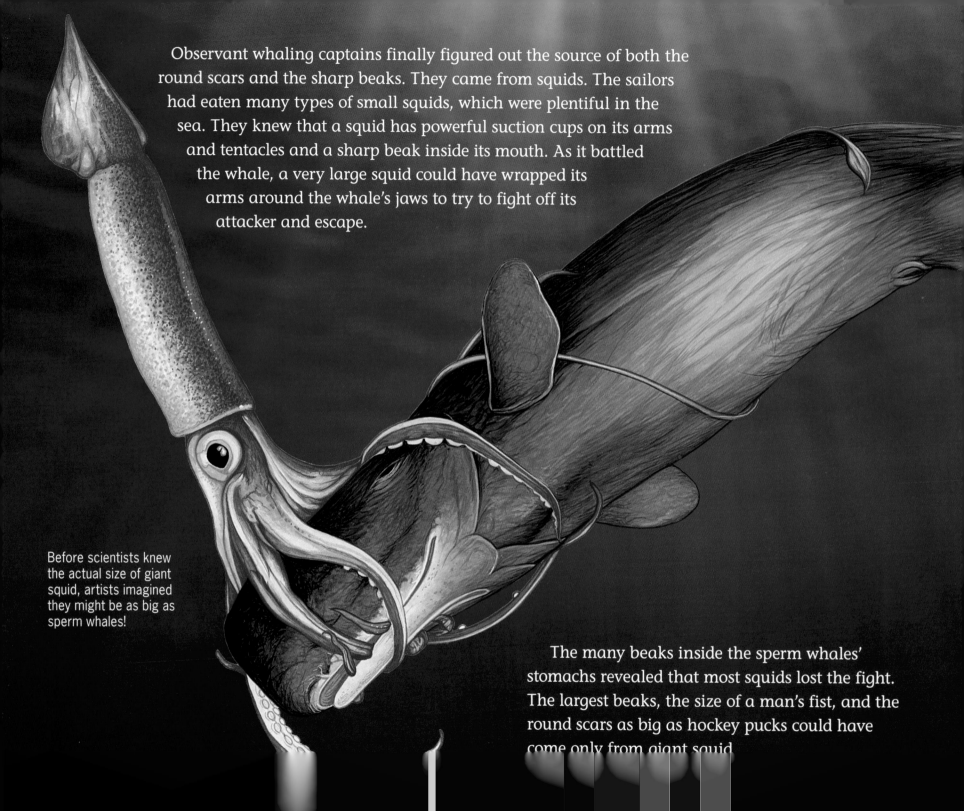

Observant whaling captains finally figured out the source of both the round scars and the sharp beaks. They came from squids. The sailors had eaten many types of small squids, which were plentiful in the sea. They knew that a squid has powerful suction cups on its arms and tentacles and a sharp beak inside its mouth. As it battled the whale, a very large squid could have wrapped its arms around the whale's jaws to try to fight off its attacker and escape.

Before scientists knew the actual size of giant squid, artists imagined they might be as big as sperm whales!

The many beaks inside the sperm whales' stomachs revealed that most squids lost the fight. The largest beaks, the size of a man's fist, and the round scars as big as hockey pucks could have come only from giant squid.

This giant squid's beak is made of chitin and is similar to crab and lobster shells.

Round scars embedded in a sperm whale's soft skin reveal that the giant squid's suckers were rimmed with small, sharp teeth.

Where would a sperm whale and a giant squid meet?

Whaling captains harpooned sperm whales when these marine mammals came to the surface to breathe. Little did the sailors know then that the whales regularly dive down to 4,000 feet (1,200 meters) or even deeper. It's there in the deep ocean that the sperm whales encounter their favorite meal, the giant squid.

Occasionally a dying giant squid was hauled up in a fishing net, or pieces of giant squid would wash ashore. In 1873 Newfoundland fishermen caught what they called "a sea monster" and showed it to their local clergyman, the Reverend Moses Harvey. In those days ministers often served as the local experts on scientific as well as spiritual matters. The Reverend Harvey persuaded the fishermen to give him the remains of the squid, which he draped over a bathtub and put on display.

It was the first complete giant squid specimen known to science.

Left: The Reverend Moses Harvey put his "sea monster" on display by carefully draping it over a bathtub to show off its many arms and tentacles.

Opposite page: Many giant squid washed up on the shores of eastern Canada in the late 1800s.

Why do giant squid sometimes wash up on shore?

Scientists know that sometimes deep, cold ocean currents change their course, moving closer to the surface. Animals that normally live in the depths, including giant squid, may be transported by wayward currents into new territory, often to warmer, shallower water closer to land. There the dramatic

differences in water temperature can kill deep-sea animals. Scientists suspect that these conditions existed at the times when dead giant squid washed ashore off the eastern coast of Canada.

A giant sqiud washed up on a New Zealand beach in 1984.

11

Meet the Squid Hunter

Despite the stories of giant squid attacking ships, scientists have learned that these beasts rarely emerge from their home at 1,600 to 3,300 feet (500 to 1,000 m) below sea surface. Even today, almost no humans have gone where giant squid reside. And sightings of these giants at the surface are rare and mysterious events.

This mystery helped inspire one person who made it his life's work to find and study these creatures.

A periwinkle and its trail—just like the ones Clyde followed as a child

Clyde Roper, giant squid hunter

It began with snails. As a child, Clyde Roper spent hours following narrow trails along the seashore in New Hampshire. The trails led him to a tiny snail, a periwinkle, plowing through the wet sand on its one slimy foot.

Clyde didn't realize until years later that these tracks in the sand were the first clues in his hunt for the giant squid. Snails and squids are related. They belong to the same group, *mollusks*, which means "soft-bodied animals." Some, such as periwinkles, have shells to retreat into. Others, such as squids, do not.

GIANT SQUID

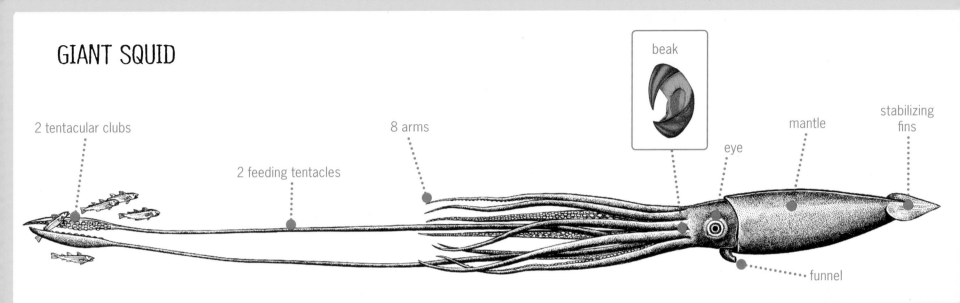

2 tentacular clubs

2 feeding tentacles

8 arms

beak

eye

mantle

stabilizing fins

funnel

But who needs a shell when you have nifty ways to escape predators and capture food? A squid can make a quick escape using jet propulsion. It shoots water out of its body through a funnel to rocket backward, like a balloon suddenly releasing its air.

A squid is an aggressive hunter, equipped with eight arms and two long feeding tentacles that it keeps tucked between its arms until it is ready to strike. Then the squid shoots out the tentacles to capture its prey and drag it to the sharp beak inside its mouth.

Some mollusks have shells. Others do not. Nudibranchs have other ways to protect themselves, such as secreting acid to discourage an attacker.

In college, Clyde studied the group of mollusks called *cephalopods*, a word that means "head-footed." He learned all he could about the many types of squids and their relatives—octopuses, cuttlefishes, and chambered nautiluses. Each member of this group has a flexible body with big eyes and a mouth surrounded by many arms. Octopuses have eight arms. Squids and cuttlefishes have eight arms plus two tentacles. But the chambered nautilus holds the record, with 80 to 100 arms!

Cephalopods are the most complex group of mollusks. The head contains the brain and large eyes, and the body holds the animal's organs: heart (most have three hearts), kidneys, liver, stomach, and gills. The gills take oxygen from the seawater as it passes through them, allowing squids and octopuses to breathe.

Like other cephalopods, the giant squid has suction cups to grab on to things. The giant squid's suckers are surrounded by small, sharp teeth that dig into the flesh of its prey. Its sharp beak has proven strong enough to bite through steel cable.

cephalopods
"head-footed"

chambered nautiluses

cuttlefishes

squids

octopuses

Why then does the sperm whale always have the advantage in a contest with the giant squid? It's because the sperm whale's mouth is ideal for capturing soft-bodied prey. It has teeth only in the bottom jaw. Those huge, cone-shaped teeth fit snugly into sockets in the upper jaw. This way the whale can hold on to victims that have no bones or shells. A giant squid doesn't stand a chance.

Get a grip! The open mouth of a sperm whale shows how it can clench a soft squid between its jaws.

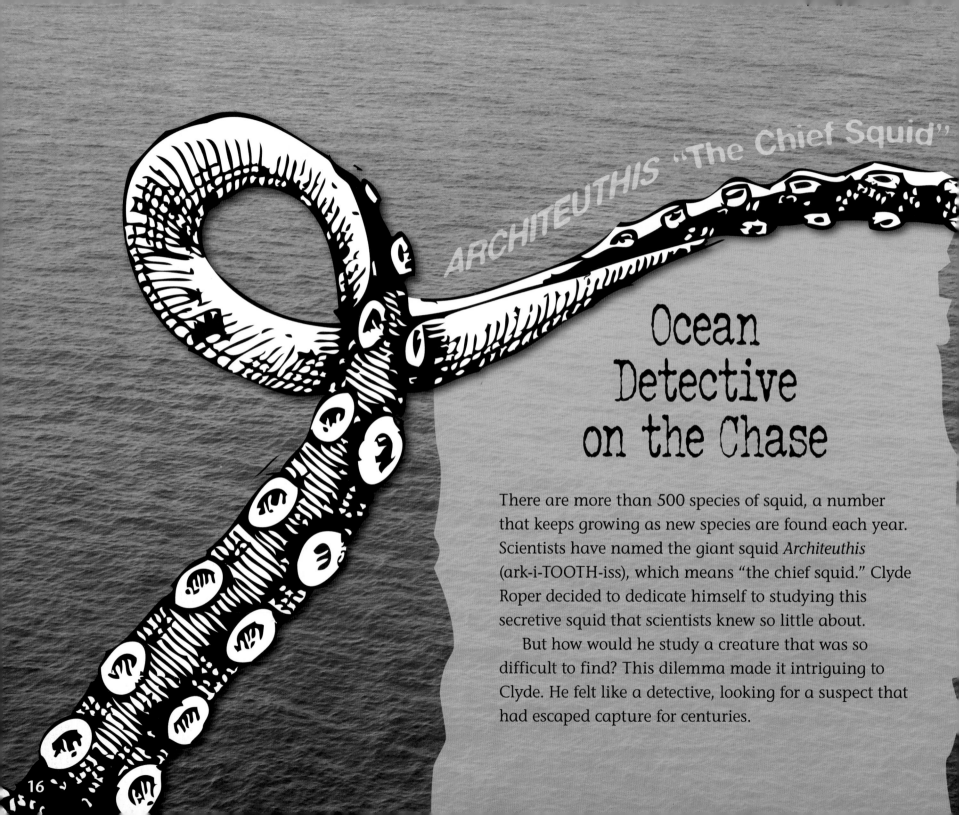

Ocean Detective on the Chase

There are more than 500 species of squid, a number that keeps growing as new species are found each year. Scientists have named the giant squid *Architeuthis* (ark-i-TOOTH-iss), which means "the chief squid." Clyde Roper decided to dedicate himself to studying this secretive squid that scientists knew so little about.

But how would he study a creature that was so difficult to find? This dilemma made it intriguing to Clyde. He felt like a detective, looking for a suspect that had escaped capture for centuries.

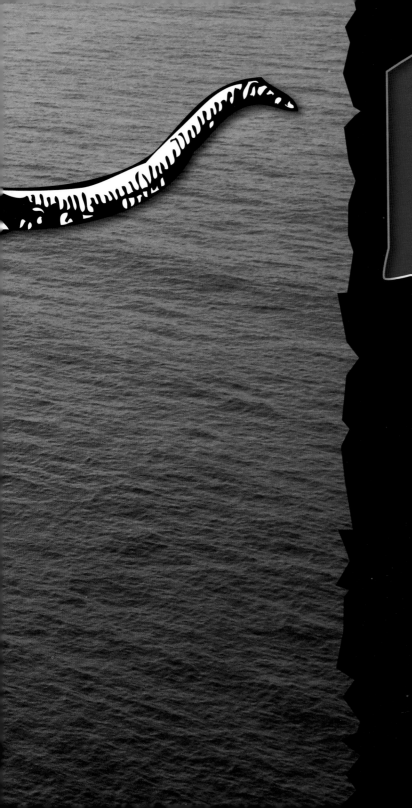

How scientists solve mysteries

Scientists make observations that lead to an idea they want to test (a hypothesis). To test the idea, they collect information or gather clues (data) by observing nature or by designing an experiment. Then, like detectives, they try to figure out what all the clues mean. Often more answers lead to more questions. Scientists don't give up if the answer is difficult to find. Unlike TV detectives who can solve a case in an hour, it sometimes takes a lifetime—or longer—to solve a scientific mystery.

A beached sperm whale gives Clyde Roper a chance to look for giant squid.

One day when Clyde was studying at the University of Miami, he got a call about a dead sperm whale that had washed ashore. Did anyone want to examine it? Absolutely! Since sperm whales were no longer hunted, this was a rare chance to try to find a modern-day link between sperm whales and giant squid. Clyde and his friends raced to the beach. They jumped into the ditch that had been dug to bury the whale's body. Armed with knives, saws, and hatchets, they cut into one stomach, then another, and then another, until they were up to their shoulders inside the whale's three stomachs. It was a messy job. But would it give them clues to the giant squid?

Clyde really gets into his work.

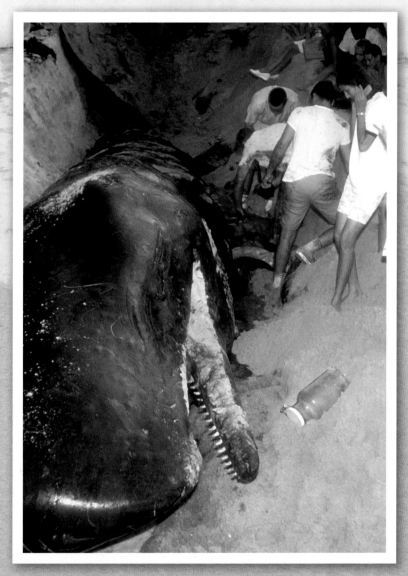

Dissecting a sperm whale carcass could teach Clyde and his fellow graduate students about the whale's favorite food.

Hours later the researchers had retrieved nearly 1,000 squid beaks. They were amazed by the huge number of squids a whale could eat, but none of the beaks belonged to a giant squid. However, they did discover many large, circular scars around the whale's mouth, proving the whale had battled and devoured giant squid during its lifetime.

Eager to clean up before getting into their car, Clyde and his friends trotted to the water's edge. They saw dozens of shark fins just beyond the surf, attracted by the smell of whale blood. Change of plans. The men had to drive back home in their blood-soaked clothes.

After years of study, Clyde Roper was now a PhD—a doctor of science. Dr. Roper was invited to join the staff of the Smithsonian Institution's Museum of Natural History in Washington, D.C. He began investigating many kinds of squids, from species the size of his thumbnail to ones nearly as tall as he was. Soon specimens of all kinds of squids arrived at the Smithsonian for Clyde to examine, including giant squid. The work only fueled his curiosity to see a live giant squid in the ocean.

southern calamari squid

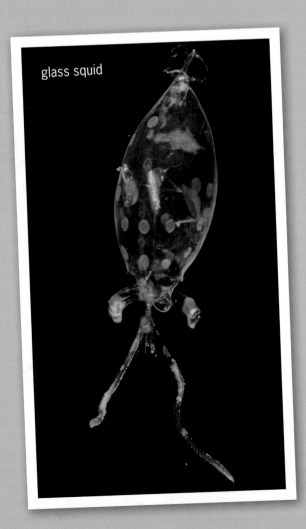

glass squid

oval squid

There are more than 500 known species of squids, with more being discovered each year.

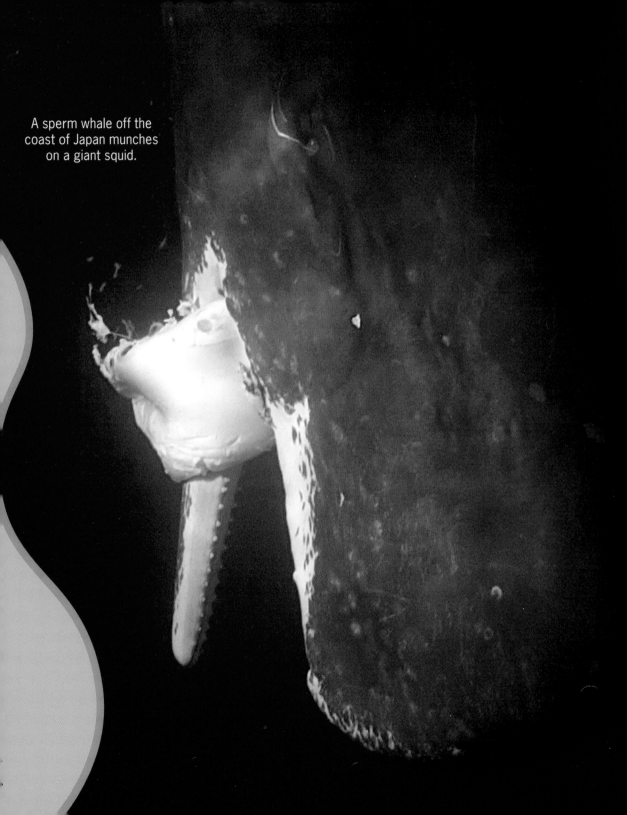

A sperm whale off the coast of Japan munches on a giant squid.

How many giant squid are there and how do we know?

Researchers have estimated the population of giant squid by counting the number of giant squid beaks found inside sperm whales' stomachs. The whales can't digest hard objects, so the beaks are usually passed out of the whales in about a week, encased in ambergris. One sperm whale may eat as many as 20,000 squids a week. Of those, perhaps only three are giants. So one sperm whale may devour about 150 giant squid a year. It's estimated that there are at least 400,000 sperm whales living in all the world's oceans. (Some whale biologists think there may be more than a million.) So how many giant squid do all those whales eat each year? That's 60 million giant squid! Of course, not all giant squid are eaten by sperm whales, so there could be many more millions of giant squid hiding deep in the world's oceans.

What Autopsies Reveal

In all of recorded history, fewer than 500 specimens of giant squid have ever been found. In more than 40 years of research, Clyde has examined nearly 100.

The largest giant squid ever recorded was reported to measure 60 feet (18 m) long. Clyde suspects that those who claimed to have found the world's largest giant squid may have stretched the squid (and the truth) a bit to make it seem longer. The largest specimen that Clyde has studied was nearly 46 feet (14 m) long. Most of the adult giant squid found have been about 25 to 33 feet (7.5 to 10 m) long. The tentacles make up two-thirds of their overall length. The giant squid ranks among the ocean's largest animals, its size exceeded only by a few species of whales and sharks.

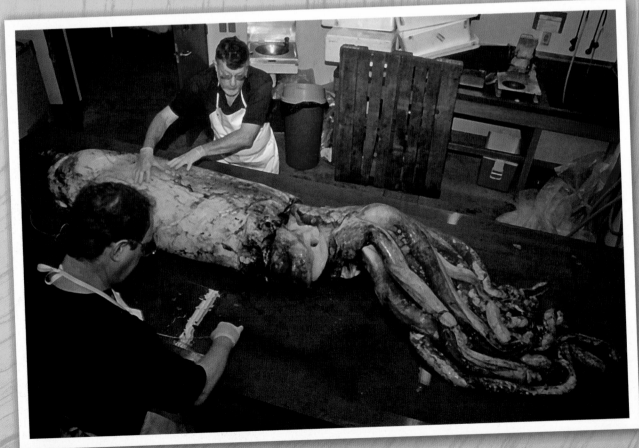

Clyde Roper (top) and Michael Sweeney examine a large giant squid that had been caught in a fisherman's net off New Zealand.

Squids, much like trees, have growth rings. Squids' rings are located in tiny ear bones called statoliths. They are called daily rings because a new ring is laid down each day. Clyde has counted the giant squid's growth rings to figure out that it lives about a year, possibly two. This tells scientists that giant squid are very fast-growing animals.

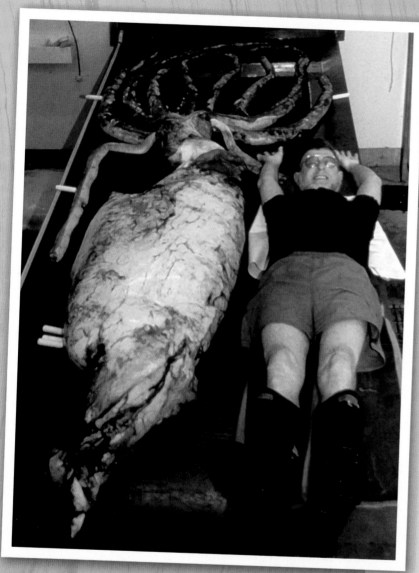

Clyde checks to see how his 6-foot (183-centimeter) frame measures up next to the mantle of a giant squid.

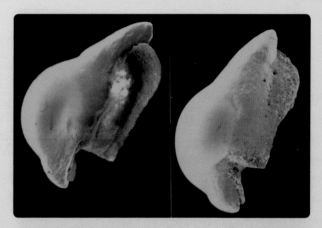

A statolith, shown in front and back views, helps a squid maintain its balance and tell it how fast it is swimming. Circular rings in statoliths can be used to estimate a squid's age.

A statolith was cut into a very thin slice to be viewed under a microscope. Each dark and light band represents one day's growth.

The adult giant squid's eyes, its most remarkable feature, are the size of car headlights. How do they penetrate the permanent darkness of the deep sea to find their prey? How far can giant squid see? Clyde wanted to answer these questions—and many more.

Clyde talked with deep-sea fishermen who had caught giant squid in their fishing nets. He examined bodies of squid that had washed up on shore. But dead or dying specimens couldn't answer the one big question that haunted Clyde: How does a giant squid behave in its natural habitat? He decided he had to find out.

The eye of a giant squid is the largest in the natural world. This one is nearly the size of Clyde's head.

Many marine animals, such as jellyfishes, glow in the dark. Why? Maybe it's to attract mates or food, scare away predators, or to find their way in the blackness of the deep ocean.

How do deep-sea creatures see in the dark?

Below a depth of 660 to 3,300 feet (200 to 1,000 m), the ocean is in permanent darkness. There the blinking lights on tiny microscopic animals look like fairy dust. They illuminate the fangs of strange, deep-sea fishes. More than three-quarters of deep-sea animals are bioluminescent—they produce their own living lights, like fireflies. Clyde wondered if giant squid also glow in the dark.

25

Seeking out the Giant Squid's Relatives

Scientists study similar animals to learn about the characteristics and behavior of elusive creatures like the giant squid. They make deductions that may help them zero in on their target.

So if Clyde couldn't yet swim with a giant squid, he would find the next best thing. He went to Mexico's western coast, where the cold waters of the Humboldt Current are home to another large squid, the Humboldt squid. A Humboldt squid can weigh as much as 100 pounds (45 kilograms) and grow to be more than 8 feet (2.4 m) long. Although not nearly as large as the other big squids, it has a reputation as a vicious killer.

At night Humboldt squid gather by the hundreds, even thousands, near the surface of the Sea of Cortez to hunt for fishes, shrimps, and other cephalopods. Fishermen there have a special name for this squid: *diablo rojo*, red devil. It earned its nickname partly because its body flashes deep red when it's caught on a fishing line, and partly because a Humboldt squid ferociously attacks bait, other Humboldt squid, and sometimes even humans.

A Humboldt squid, known locally as the red devil, devours another Humboldt squid in the Sea of Cortez.

Clyde learned first-hand about Humboldt squid attacks when he and a film crew from National Geographic accompanied the fishermen one night. The fishermen caught the Humboldt squid on special fishing lures called jigs that allow the captured squid to slip off the line as soon as it is flipped aboard the boat. When a large female squid was caught on a jig, Clyde put on his wetsuit and scuba tank and dove underwater. Clyde moved in to get a closer look. He was staring into her open mouth when the squid suddenly nipped Clyde with her fist-sized beak and jetted away.

After several hours of observing and filming more Humboldt squid—from a safer distance—Clyde climbed back into the boat, exhausted. He peeled off his wetsuit and discovered blood spurting from a deep wound where the squid had bitten him. He still has the scar on his thigh to remind him he might well have suffered a worse fate. Watching the Humboldt squid helped Clyde imagine how the giant squid might hunt and capture its food. It also made him wonder what an encounter with a giant squid might be like if it is as fierce as the red devil.

Clyde holds up a Humboldt squid like the one that took a bite out of his leg. The wound can be seen on his thigh.

wound from squid bite

The open beak of a Humboldt squid is a scary sight, especially if you encounter it underwater at night.

There is another gigantic squid ...

A squid known as the colossal squid is found in the cold, deep waters around Antarctica. If squids were athletes, the giant squid would be a long, lean basketball player. The colossal squid would be a football player. It's much heavier and bulkier than *Architeuthis*. The first colossal squid, with strange, fanglike suckers on its tentacles, was discovered in 1925 inside—you guessed it—the stomach of a sperm whale. Scientists have counted the number of colossal squid beaks found inside the stomachs of sperm whales. They have estimated that colossal squid make up three-quarters of the diet of the sperm whales that feed in the Southern Ocean, which surrounds Antarctica.

The British sailing ship *Silvery Light* served as Clyde's research vessel on a National Geographic expedition off the Azores in the Atlantic Ocean.

A squid biologist examines a colossal squid ... a BIG job! Compared to the giant squid, its body is longer but its arms are shorter.

Diving Deeper

Inspired by what he learned from the giant squid's cousins, Clyde was even more determined to search for his giant ... alive. He launched a National Geographic expedition to the Azores Islands in the middle of the Atlantic Ocean, where sperm whales go to feed. The sperm whale would show him the way.

Clyde knew he couldn't dive deep enough to follow the whales. Giant squid live far deeper than a scuba diver can go, so Clyde had to find other ways to seek his giant. He enlisted the help of National Geographic photographer Greg Marshall, the inventor of the "Crittercam." This special video camera can be attached to sea animals, such as dolphins, seals, and sea turtles, to record their underwater journeys.

The Crittercam, invented by a National Geographic engineer, has been used to follow many different creatures, including penguins, into the wild.

Scientists used a big blue suction cup to attach the Crittercam to a sperm whale's head.

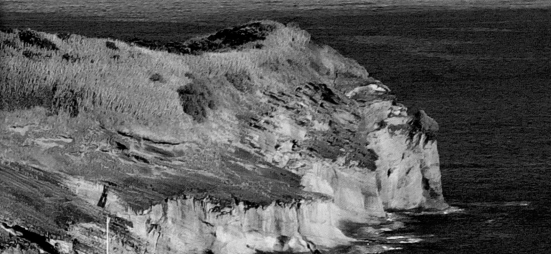

31

How do you fasten a camera to a 100,000-pound wild animal?

Very carefully!

When the researchers were ready to attach the camera, they quietly paddled an inflatable kayak toward a whale resting just under the water's surface. The whale remained surprisingly calm as they attached the camera to its head with a suction cup. A video camera, depth recorder, and audio recorder mounted on the suction cup recorded the whale's dive. An hour later the camera was released from the whale. A pinging sound led the searchers to the camera, floating in the water.

The excited scientists hauled the Crittercam on board and played the video. Would they see the first glimpse of a giant squid in action? The whale had descended to 2,600 feet (800 m). The lights on the camera could penetrate only a few feet into the darkness at that depth. But the sound recorder allowed the scientists to hear the calls of distant whales. The sperm whale returned their calls. Gradually more and more sounds collected around the whale.

Clyde's team could hear the whales greeting each other. Perhaps they were saying, "I found a great place to get squid!"

They sent the Crittercam down seven more times on that expedition. Clyde learned a great deal about the giant squid's habitat and its predators, but he still hadn't found his squid.

What about tracking the creatures that the giant squid eats?

A small kayak may not seem the safest way to approach a sperm whale resting on the surface, but the scientists worried that a motor boat would scare it away.

Follow the Food

A fellow scientist told Clyde he'd found deep-sea fish called orange roughy inside the stomachs of dead giant squid. So Clyde led an oceanographic cruise to the underwater canyon where fishermen net these fish. Sperm whales also gather there. Clyde used an Autonomous Underwater Vehicle (AUV), a miniature sub controlled from the surface by computer. He felt as if he were swimming among the fishes as he directed the sub from the control room of the research ship.

Clyde learned more about what the giant squid eat, and the other animals that live at those great depths, but he did not find the giant squid.

Are giant squid good to eat?

Clyde loves to eat squid, which is called calamari when prepared as food. No one had ever tasted a giant squid, so Clyde, always curious, decided he should taste a specimen that one of his friends had stored in his fridge. "It was very, very bitter," he recalls. The meat was analyzed and the scientists discovered the muscles contain a chemical similar to one in our urine!

The scientists launch the *Odyssey*, an AUV equipped with a Crittercam in the nose.

Ancient fish, ancient forests

Orange roughy are some of the longest-lived fishes in the ocean. Left undisturbed, these fish may live to be more than 100 years old. The orange roughy inhabit huge groves of ancient "tree" corals up to 33 feet (10 m) tall and more than 1,000 years old. Corals, though they may look like plants, are animals—relatives of jellyfishes and sea anemones.

Orange roughy and the coral "forests" are being wiped out by deep-sea trawlers. Their heavy nets mow down the ancient corals to scoop up the orange roughy, which are sold as "deep-sea perch." Before long, the orange roughy—and this food for the giant squid—will be gone.

On Clyde's next research trip, he and a crew from Discovery Channel used a manned submarine, the *Deep Rover*. The sub explored an underwater canyon off the coast of New Zealand, where another favorite food of giant squid lives: hoki fish. Sperm whales know that too. Young sperm whales go there to gorge on giant squid and other kinds of deep-sea squids.

Clyde figured that giant squid might be attracted to the bioluminescent light given off by most deep-sea animals, so he draped the sub with light sticks, like those that trick-or-treaters carry on Halloween. A pilot inside the tiny sub maneuvered the *Deep Rover*. Continual images from several video cameras beamed back to Clyde in the ship's control room as he watched expectantly.

Clyde's team saw a blue-green bioluminescent light show from the many deep-sea creatures. But the giant squid remained hidden.

However, with each new expedition, Clyde learned new things about squid predators and squid prey. He learned about the giant squid's ecosystem—the area it lives in and all it contains. All of these findings provided more and more clues to solving the secrets of the giant squid.

The New Zealand ship *Kaharoa* carried Clyde to Kaikoura Canyon, a deep trench off the coast of New Zealand.

Clyde sits in a small submarine, the *Deep Rover*, shortly before it descends into the deep waters where giant squid lurk.

The *Deep Rover* carried several video cameras, both inside and out, ready to capture a giant squid on film.

Discovering more about the deep-sea ecosystem can tell us about squid and, more importantly, the future of giant squid. Fishing boats drag heavy nets across the ocean floor and destroy the habitats of many bottom-dwelling animals that giant squid depend on for food. Clyde worries that the ocean food web is threatened by overfishing. If the food supply of the giant squid disappears, this in turn will take away a main food source of the sperm whale.

Clyde shared his findings with others who study giant squid, a small group of scientists called teuthologists. Though they are spread all around the globe, they are bound together by their passion for "the chief."

Clyde and his colleagues had to find a way to let the world know about the giant squid. They hoped more people would care about the giant squid if they could see one living peacefully in its natural habitat. They wanted to show the world that these "monsters" are fascinating creatures vital to the ocean environment.

The long-finned squid, found off the coast of Maine, is a popular species used in preparing calamari.

How to have a healthy ocean

"Cephalopods," says Clyde, "are great examples of biodiversity." This is because, as a group, they are spread all over the world, from shallow tropical reefs to the great depths of the ocean. A squid from Maine will look a lot like a squid from California. But they are slightly different because of their different habitats and living conditions, enough so that they will not be able to mate and have offspring. They are known as different species.

"Preserving this fascinating variety of life is important for keeping all life in the oceans healthy," Clyde says.

Taking the Bait

A Japanese doctor of zoology, Tsunemi Kubodera, continued the search using Clyde's documented evidence that sperm whales lead to giant squid. Dr. Kubodera chose to study an area off the Japanese coast where sperm whales come to feed each year from September to December. He programmed a camera to take a flash picture every 30 seconds and attached it to a long fishing line. Hooks on the line were baited with chopped shrimps and squids, in the hope of luring a giant squid into camera range.

They lowered the fishing line into the deep and waited ...

... and waited.

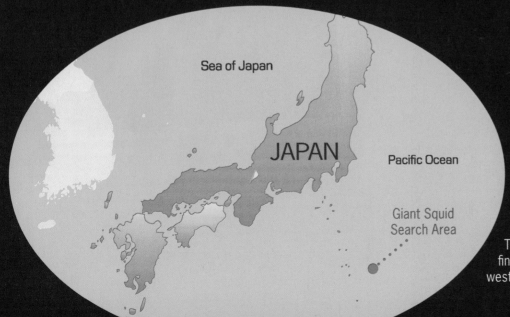

Tsunemi Kubodera's expedition to find a giant squid centered in the western Pacific Ocean.

diagram not to scale

Pole & flag

Floats

Main line

1,300–3,300 feet
(400–1,000m)

Small light

Camera +
depth logger

5 feet
(1.5m)

Fishing line

3.3 feet
(1m)

Hook +
bait squid

1.6 feet

1.6 feet
(0.5m)

Shrimp bait bag

1.6 feet

Weighted squid jig + bait squid

A deep-sea camera used baited fishing line to lure giant squid.

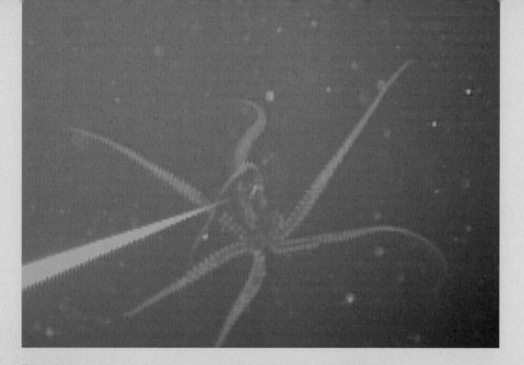

Kubodera made 23 trips over three years to the area and repeated the experiment. Finally a giant squid grabbed the baited hook! For four hours the captured squid twisted and turned. Sometimes it attacked the bait. Other times it pulled away, trying to escape. The camera took 556 underwater images of the squid before it managed to break free, leaving a tentacle 18 feet (5.5 m) long embedded on the hook. When the team brought the tentacle on board, the large suckers grabbed on to the deck of the boat, and then on to Kubodera's fingers.

Two of the hundreds of underwater photos Kubodera took as the giant squid struggled to free itself from the hook. The images, though fuzzy because they were enlarged, are thrilling to see as they capture a historic moment in ocean science.

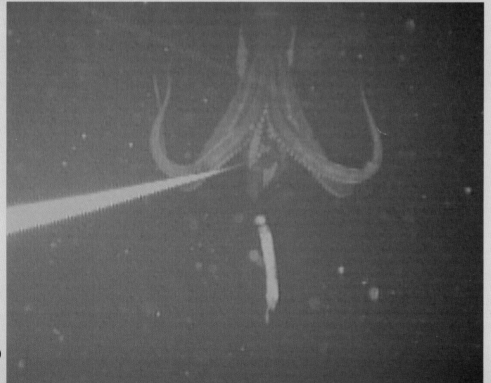

The squid's 18-foot (5.5-m) tentacle caught on the hook

These first photographs of a living giant squid were released in 2005. Clyde celebrated along with the rest of the "squid world." Examining the photos, Clyde saw that a giant squid is far more active than anyone had expected. Despite its huge size, it was not a sluggish creature waiting for food to come near. It made Clyde recall his encounter with another aggressive hunter, the Humboldt squid.

Why didn't the giant squid leave circular scars on the scientist?

The scars on sperm whales are made by a giant squid fighting to avoid the whale's jaws during a fierce but short battle for survival—which the squid usually loses. The giant squid that Kubodera captured was caught in about 3,000 feet (900 m) of water, and it dragged the heavy camera rig and cable all the way up to about 2,000 feet (600 m) before it broke loose. "By the time the snagged tentacle broke off and the squid escaped, it must have been a pretty exhausted calamari!" said Clyde. The squid latched on to Kubodera's fingers, but didn't have the strength left to cause harm.

The suckers at the end of a giant squid's tentacles can grasp objects.

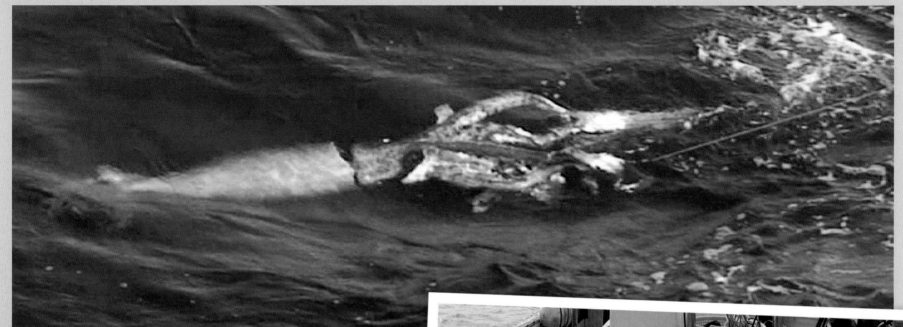

The first video footage of a living giant squid was taken as it was caught on a fishing line baited with a smaller species of squid (top and opposite page).

Two years after Kubodera's photos, another breakthrough! His team recorded the world's first video of a live giant squid. They caught the squid at a depth of 2,133 feet (650 m) and hauled it to the surface. As the team worked to bring it on board, the thrashing squid fought against the fishing line and shot powerful jets of water from its funnel. These first-hand observations confirmed for scientists that the giant squid is indeed a strong swimmer, an active predator, and a fierce fighter.

Tsunemi Kubodera, PhD, sits next to the giant squid he captured to study. It is now on display at the National Museum of Natural History in Tokyo.

The Hunt Continues

The world has learned so much about ocean life since Clyde's days of tracking snails on the beach. He and his fellow teuthologists have discovered and shared a great deal about giant squid and other ocean mysteries.

- ✓ We know what giant squid eat.

- ✓ We know what eats them.

- ✓ We know more about how to find them.

- ✓ We know more about their distant and mysterious ecosystem.

- ✓ We know what they look like, alive and active.

But there is so much more we need to find out about this legendary creature. We still know so little about its behavior and biology. Although Clyde Roper has retired from the Smithsonian, his determination to find a living giant squid continues, because he has many more questions yet to answer.

- ? Do giant squid gather in huge groups to court and mate like some other squids do?

- ? Do they protect their eggs until they hatch as mother octopuses do?

- ? Do they squirt ink? Is the ink bioluminescent?

- ? How strong are their arms and tentacles?

A giant squid is one of the most popular exhibits in the Sant Ocean Hall of the Smithsonian Museum of Natural History in Washington, D.C.

Scientists hope someday to see at least one of the estimated millions of giant squid, swimming, eating, courting, fighting, and just being itself in its home in the inky blackness of the deep sea.

Clyde Roper often stops by the Sant Ocean Hall in the Museum of Natural History to visit the male and female giant squid that are on display there. Encased in Plexiglas coffins, floating in a special liquid that preserves them for all to see, they almost seem like creatures from another planet.

But Clyde knows better. "Sea monsters are real," he says, "and I have seen them."

Could we keep a giant squid in an aquarium?

Scientists would love to capture a giant squid to study it. But could we keep it alive in captivity? Richard Lerner, the curator of fishes at the National Aquarium in Baltimore, Maryland, doubts it. "There are so many unanswered questions: Will it eat anything else in the tank with it? Will it accept dead food? Can it live in shallow water, since it is used to the pressure of the deep sea? Giant squid live in very cold temperatures, so the chiller would have to be immense. Giant squid aren't designed to handle walls. If it tried to jet propel backwards, it would crash into the walls of a tank. There is no tank in the world that could hold it."

Glossary

ambergris waxy substance found in the digestive system of sperm whales

biodiversity variety of life in genetics, species, and ecosystems

bioluminescent able to produce light as a living thing; certain animals, such as fireflies and deep-sea fishes, are bioluminscent

cephalopod member of an advanced group of mollusks, characterized by head, big brain, arms with suckers, and beak

depth recorder a machine that measures the depths of the ocean

ecosystem living things and their environments functioning as a unit

funnel a tubelike structure on a squid or octopus used to eject water from the body sac during breathing and locomotion; the animal forces water out of the funnel to move backward rapidly

habitat the place where an animal or plant grows or lives

mollusk an animal belonging to the mollusk group (Phylum Mollusca), which includes snails, clams, octopuses, cuttlefishes, chambered nautiluses, and squids; while they are all soft-bodied animals, some mollusks have strong shells and others do not

statolith the ear bone of a squid, which helps the animal maintain its balance underwater

teuthologist scientist who studies squids

Explore Further

Websites

http://seawifs.gsfc.nasa.gov/squid.html
In Search of Giant Squid, part of the Ocean Planet
Exhibition, Smithsonian Museum of Natural History

http://animals.nationalgeographic.com/animals/
invertebrates/giant-squid.html/
National Geographic Wild

http://squid.tepapa.govt.nz/build-a-squid/interactive
Build a Squid, part of the Colossal Squid Exhibition,
Museum of New Zealand Te Papa Tongarewa

Books

Emmer, Rick. *Kraken: Fact or Fiction?* Creature Scene
Investigation. New York: Chelsea House, 2010.

Markle, Sandra. *Outside and Inside Giant Squid.*
New York: Walker, 2003.

Matsen, Brad. *The Incredible Hunt for the Giant Squid.*
Incredible Deep-Sea Adventures. Berkeley Heights, N.J.:
Enslow Publishers, 2003.

McKerley, Jennifer. *The Kraken.* Monsters. Detroit, Mich.:
KidHaven Press, 2008.

Newquist, H.P. *Here There Be Monsters: The Legendary
Kraken and the Giant Squid.* Boston: Houghton
Mifflin, 2010.

A Note from the Authors:

The idea for this project was hatched when Clyde Roper graciously agreed
to fly to Maine (in a snowstorm, as it turned out) to give a talk to a group of
marine educators. He granted many hours of interviews, shared his library
of photographs, and enlisted more from a worldwide network of fellow
teuthologists, photographers, and illustrators with whom he has collaborated.

Many thanks are owed to Ingrid Roper, the "keeper" of the giant squid
archives, photographs, and the giant squid hunter himself. Thanks also to
Michael Vecchione of NOAA Systematics Laboratory at the Smithsonian
Institution's Museum of Natural History for reviewing the manuscript, and
to Jaime Ramsay and Rich Lerner, who patiently answered many questions
about maintaining cephalopods in captivity.

Thanks, too, to our editors and designers at Capstone Press, who
encouraged and nurtured us throughout: Kristen Mohn, Sarah Bennett,
Deirdre Barton, and Laura Manthe.

Index

About the Authors:

When Mary Cerullo turned 13, she decided she wanted to become an oceanographer. Later on she discovered she liked teaching and writing about the ocean as much as studying it. Describing herself as a "science interpreter," Mary explains scientific research and environmental issues in ways that the public can appreciate. As associate director of Friends of Casco Bay, she helps to protect the frigid but fascinating waters off the coast of Maine. This is Mary's 16th children's book on the ocean.

Clyde Roper, PhD, is a marine biologist who has specialized in squids ever since he was in graduate school long ago. He has spent his whole career at the Smithsonian Institution's Museum of Natural History. There he has studied small squids that live in the deep oceans, but he is also fascinated by the largest squid of them all. Clyde has conducted several expeditions in search of a living giant squid in its natural habitat. Clyde continues his research, writing and lecturing as an emeritus zoologist at the Smithsonian.